ALABASTER

Library of Congress Cataloging-in-Publication Data is available upon request.
Library of Congress Control Number: 2020941392

ISBN: 978-1-952357-04-6

Contact:
hello@alabasterco.com
www.alabasterco.com

Alabaster Co explores the intersection of creativity, beauty, and faith. Founded
in 2016. Based in Los Angeles.

ON BEAUTY AND FAITH

CONTENTS

———

INTRODUCTION

What is beauty? For most, beauty describes a store's cosmetics section or a passing compliment. It is often associated with words like *attractive, pretty,* or *handsome.* It is an ideal we aspire to, and a pleasure we occasionally enjoy.

We all have experienced beauty in these ways. Still, these common categories hardly ever engage the incredible depth, significance, and possibilities of beauty. As we encounter and discover God, we are inevitably led to further unpack our sense of beauty. The scriptures are full of stories, revelations, and teachings that can only be described as—*beautiful.*

This sacred connection between beauty and God is especially relevant for our world today. As a society, we often describe God as *true* and *good.* We use *beauty* less often—and we struggle to articulate the intuitive relationship between it and the things of God: calling, spirituality, mission, and more. This book serves as a starting point to bridge the gap.

The word *beautiful* reveals itself most notably in Mark 14:1-11, *The Story of the Woman with the Alabaster Jar.* Amid the hostility of the onlookers, Jesus says: "Leave her alone, why are you bothering her? She has done a *beautiful* thing to me." The word he uses for *beauty,* in the original Greek, is *kalos.* The depth of *kalos* escapes us. It can be defined as moral goodness or aesthetic beauty, and in this case, *beautiful* as an outward sign of an inward goodness.

What compels Jesus to single out this act as *kalos*? What does the woman's act mean? Why are onlookers filled with disgust? In this book, we explore the woman's act and its quality of beauty. We delve into the larger questions and themes in this story: art, identity, generosity, vulnerability, mystery, justice, and changing the world. And we meditate on the vast importance of beauty in our spiritual practice, creative work, and collective future.

Through this exploration, we hope to cultivate a deeper understanding of beauty and its implications for our lives. May it lead us more fully into the presence of God. Amen.

THE STORY OF THE WOMAN
WITH THE ALABASTER JAR

[1] Now the Passover and the Festival of Unleavened Bread were only two days away, and the chief priests and the teachers of the law were scheming to arrest Jesus secretly and kill him. [2] "But not during the festival," they said, "or the people may riot." [3] While he was in Bethany, reclining at the table in the home of Simon the Leper, a woman came with an alabaster jar of very expensive perfume, made of pure nard. She broke the jar and poured the perfume on his head. [4] Some of those present were saying indignantly to one another, "Why this waste of perfume? [5] It could have been sold for more than a year's wages and the money given to the poor." And they rebuked her harshly. [6] "Leave her alone," said Jesus. "Why are you bothering her? She has done a beautiful thing to me. [7] The poor you will always have with you, and you can help them any time you want. But you will not always have me. [8] She did what she could. She poured perfume on my body beforehand to prepare for my burial. [9] Truly I tell you, wherever the gospel is preached throughout the world, what she has done will also be told, in memory of her." [10] Then Judas Iscariot, one of the Twelve, went to the chief priests to betray Jesus to them. [11] They were delighted to hear this and promised to give him money. So he watched for an opportunity to hand him over.

– Mark 14:1-11 NIV

01

On Beauty
and Art

What makes art beautiful? Creatives, philosophers, and mystics have always sought to explore and answer this question. Beauty is universally felt—and yet perpetually escapes our paradigms. When artists follow Jesus, this question takes on new dimensions.

The exploration of beauty in art has long been embedded within our spiritual history. Leonardo Da Vinci's *Last Supper* or Michelangelo's *Creation of Adam*, for example, depicted divine and higher ideals—they continue to be hailed as beautiful today. But grandiose Renaissance-era paintings and baroque, embellished cathedrals are no longer our norm. As times have shifted, artistic "beauty" is not so rigidly defined. In the creative spirit, modern art provides chambers for rediscovery and redefinition. As a culture and as creatives, we are tasked with forging fresh frameworks to answer the question of beauty today.

Though this is a lofty, multilayered conversation, the scriptures provide deep meaning to ground it. In Mark 14, the story of the unnamed woman with the alabaster jar serves as a point of departure for our collective understanding of beauty and art.

FEEDING OUR SOULS

Humans are more than physical creatures; we are *soul* beings. Just as our body experiences hunger and requires feeding, play, and rest, our souls need similar nourishment and care as well. Without it, we do not inhabit the totality of human experience. We instead become detached, disembodied, and divided. Without soul care, our physical lives and reality appear stale and purposeless. But with it, our souls guide us and our communities into the new life that Jesus often spoke of.

We do not find much "soul food" in our industrialized world today. Our culture is utilitarian-forward and fast-paced, bent on accumulating capital and producing goods. This is not necessarily wrong, but we should remember that the soul was never designed to thrive in such a context. We cannot reduce the soul to a means of production or a fuel tank to shuttle our bodies between to-do items. Rather, the soul is a world within us—brimming with meaning, life, and reason for even moving in the first place. And art, in its many purposes, has a vital role in *feeding* our souls.

In this story, the unnamed woman creates *performance* art. She moves her body into an unlikely space, using alabaster and spikenard as articles of anointing. The act is a multi-sensory artistic experience: the clatter of alabaster fragments falling on the floor, the penetrating smell of perfume, and the glimmering droplets of oil coating his skin and hair. And though profoundly sensory, her art is also soulful. It reaches beyond the physical, and touches deeper realities.

When the woman breaks the jar on Jesus' head, she is doing more than anointing him: she, quite literally, shatters the utility and value of the jar. The jar can no longer be used as a dowry. The jar can no longer be sold for money or a noble cause. The woman renders it *useless*, subverting the physical worlds of reason and function.

This is the role of the artist. We are called to create and use things in the physical world to move people beyond the physical. We are invited to feed souls. Pencils are merely graphite—a crystalline form of carbon. Canvases are nothing but strands of cotton, plainly woven together. Singing is the result of vibrating ligaments in our larynx. We artists deal with utterly physical things. And yet, it is our sacred duty to translate these physical materials into symbol, meaning, and nourishment for the human soul.

It follows, of course, that artists must be first to embody soulful living before creatively calling others to do so. We are to be thoroughly and reflectively immersed in our inner lives as well, feeding our souls with regular prayer, contemplation, and play. As we do, we receive nutrients for the creative journey. We can paint, sing, and perform beyond the physical, because we ourselves have traveled there. And in doing so, we create art that is beautiful.

FUTURE-MAKING

The burdens of everyday living give us little time or space to be people of optimism. Individually, we are weighed down by obligations, toils, and limitations. Collectively, communities are broken, steeped in poverty and inequality. The world of *Shalom*—what theologian Walter Brueggemann calls a "communal flourishing of peace and justice" [1]—feels far away.

Amidst these realities, it is the artist's role to remind us that beauty is still all around us. That *Shalom* is indeed a future worth fighting for—but also a *present* worth accessing. The artist helps us see beyond our bleak realities into what is still possible. We give the world slivers of hope. We lead them, along with ourselves, into the optimism we cannot yet see.

When we engage in art-making, we are involved in future-making. We are showing people a new way of living. This divine privilege is what gives art the opportunity to create beauty.

Art Leads

No matter the piece or practice we prefer, we are always leading people toward something with our art. We must regularly ask ourselves: what are we leading them toward? What future are

we making? We might hope it involves giving, thriving, and flourishing—rather than despair and dispassion. Our chosen aesthetic need not be overly cheerful or bright, but we ought to make in a way that ultimately orients our world toward restoration. Through our art, we show the possibility of what could be. Through our art, we stand on the frontlines of making and calling forth *Shalom*.

"Truly I tell you, wherever the gospel is preached throughout the world, what she has done will also be told, in memory of her." – Mark 14:9 NIV

In this story, the woman leads us into a more beautiful future. Her performance bursts with generosity, vulnerability, and courage. Jesus acknowledges her art, making a statement of the future that is intended for us, today. He understands and elevates her art as precious. It will reverberate into the lives of future generations. As artists today, we stand in the legacy and example of this unnamed woman. She is our predecessor. And we follow her work, making things that will echo the good news of beauty for generations to come.

Encountering Resistance

Not everyone will be ready to enter our imaginative futures. Humans are habitual creatures, resistant to change. We obsess over structures, routines, and patterns. These are not bad things. In many ways, they help us function and sustain through a changing world. However, beautiful futures cannot be realized or inhabited when we are fixed in the status quo.

When we encounter the woman's performance art with the alabaster jar, we have the gift of perspective. We grasp its significance. Jesus' death, burial, and resurrection have already happened. We know how the story ends. But, for those in the room that day, there is no such perspective. They are stuck in their old, isolated ways of seeing the world. Can we blame them?

Jesus sees beyond our current paradigms, and he invites us to do the same. He sees that the woman is preparing him for his future-death. He sees this moment's significance in a global future that the others in the room cannot comprehend. And he sees beauty.

Future-making is a difficult task. As we strive towards beauty-making, we will inevitably unsettle individuals, cultures, and systems. In these moments, we must remember God's promise.

"The Lord himself goes before you and will be with you; he will never leave you nor forsake you. Do not be afraid; do not be discouraged." – Deuteronomy 31:8 NIV

Wherever we find ourselves, God has personally gone ahead of us. Jesus is the ultimate future-maker. We can never outpace him. As we co-create the future, we partner with the Holy Spirit to reimagine, re-work, and restore the world through our art.

BEAUTY CONNECTS

Beautiful art connects. Rather than ripping apart, beauty bends everything toward inclusivity and reconciliation. When we encounter beautiful art, we become *connected*: to ourselves, to humanity, and to the divine.

Connecting to Self

The woman with the alabaster jar is deeply connected to herself. In her art-making, she immerses herself holistically into her creative practice. Her body detaches itself from gender norms, the petty rebuke of the crowd, and the alleged waste of her materials. She instead looks inward, silently connected with Jesus. Her performance is best described as bold. Her inner contentment, resolve, and love propel her to create in an unfiltered way.

Art can open our hearts and souls to our truest selves. Artist Agnes Martin says, "But with regard to the inner life of each of us it may be of great significance... If we can know our response, see in ourselves what we have received from a work, that is the way to the understanding of truth and all beauty." [2]

Art-making is hardly ever a logical, linear process. It is full of twists and turns, setbacks and small-wins—it is a process predicated on exploration and discovery. And if we are patient, committed, and passionate about the process, we will surely discover moments of beauty. And we will come to more intimately know and befriend ourselves.

The experience of knowing and connecting with oneself unequivocally requires stillness and silence. Henri Nouwen, a Dutch Catholic priest, writes, "Solitude is not a private therapeutic place. Rather, it is the place of conversion, the place where the old self dies and the new self is born." [3]

Our world is replete with noise. As artists, we are attuned—in small and large ways—to the opinions of others. Yet, as followers of Jesus, we begin our art-making detached from the noise—and connected to ourselves. In silence and solitude, we begin to hear and feed our souls. And our creative practice begins in the original creative practice: our own making in the image of God.

Connecting to Humanity

We live in a fractured, hurt, and divided society. Groups mobilize against groups. Communities stand against communities. In this highly polarized world, the artist is invited to make work that connects humanity together.

Artists are inherent bridge-builders. We are purveyors of mutuality, relationship, and interdependence. It is typical for artists to live on the frayed edges of various groups, cultures, and communities,

familiar with the fate of never fitting in. And as we live on these margins, we artists face a unique choice.

We can choose bitterness and resentment, creating work that reflects our own dissension and the gaping ruptures of our world. Or, we can view our edge-lives as a gift, using our talents and abilities to make work that becomes a bridge for the various edges we occupy. We can mend differences and, ultimately, heal wounds.

In this story, the woman bridges communities together. Through her art, she—a woman, lowly regarded in her society—is connected with a male Jew and rabbi, Jesus. She also connects with future generations, as Jesus declares her significance. And in an unlikely way, she is connected to the judgmental, disgusted onlookers. Of course, their reaction is marked by disdain. But her performance calls to them, across the divide that they cannot see past. It beckons them to see beauty. It urges them to deeper love, generosity, and mystery. And while they do not receive or reciprocate her gift, it nonetheless connects her to them as an unlikely teacher. We are similarly invited to make art that connects rather than divides, that is in the service of others, that shows the beauty in all of humanity.

Connecting to God

As humans, we receive art through our physical senses. We see, hear, smell, taste, and touch art. And yet, we almost always perceive art to be far more than merely a physical experience. Art has the power to penetrate our souls, to break down our guarded hearts, and to give us new perspective.

In this story, the woman literally interacts with the divine. Through the humble physicality of the jar, the potent perfume, the suffusing oil—the divine is revealed. Through this anointing, the woman acknowledges Jesus as *Messiah*, the King of the Jews. She joins in the legacy of Samuel anointing Saul and David as kings, offering a spiritual and political revealing of the Savior.

This same "revealing of the divine" is offered to all of us who make. Of the many ills rising from our disembodied, disconnected reality, our distance from God is the worst. We are quick to feel this distance. Our physical senses experience simple glimpses and moments—fragments of a divine God and world that we long for.

It is the role of the artist to piece these fragments together, and discover the God who is in everything. We need not be explicit or obvious in our depictions of God—but we do bear a responsibility to demonstrate that the divine is in "everyday," "everywhere" things. As we feed souls, create futures, and make connections through our art, we ultimately give people eyes and ears to perceive the God who is all around us. This is a holy work. Amen.

02

On Beauty
and Identity

Any exploration of beauty inevitably involves *people*. Today, "beauty" is most associated with glamor, cosmetics, and aesthetics. Before a sculpture or sunset, the word "beauty" first reminds many of a person or appearance.

With these associations, beauty can be interpreted as a lifelong and ill-fated pursuit. And we are its unyielding pursuers, achingly awaiting the promised moment when we finally arrive as we aspire to be—*beautiful*.

This empty pursuit consumes itself in routines, subscriptions, and treatments. Beauty is embodied not in identities or relationships, but as an outcome that we work for. It chains itself to a fickle culture and changing world, to emerging trends and popular styles. We accept this, and yet always ache with hunger for more. In Mark 14, Jesus and the unnamed woman offer us a new understanding of beauty.

ENDING OUR PURSUIT

We are fated to search for beauty in ourselves. The first byproduct of sin was shame in our appearance, which God originally deemed *good*. Since then, we have been keenly attuned to our flaws. We have an innate desire to see ourselves as beautiful, and for others to recognize it as well.

For some, standards of beauty are not things we decide—but are always subject to. We stand outside its door, longing to find ourselves inside its walls. And we shift by the day—inside to outside, fashionable to dated, and admirable to laughable. We calculate what others fancy in us, and adjust accordingly. We swing ourselves between anxiety, pride, and jealousy, hurling ourselves into toxic, hopeless pursuits. For others positioned with power and privilege, we do make and define standards of beauty. Even then, we still bear this baggage. We cannot think of beauty any other way.

If our worldly experience of beauty is anything, it is often *exhausting*. And yet, it constantly eclipses our lives. We must have a better theology, relationship, and lived experience with beauty as identity.

What if beauty extended beyond how we look? What if we could enjoy beauty in a way that was healthy and humble, rather than commodified and objectified? What if we could discover a beauty in ourselves that was stable, trustworthy—even finished?

In this story, others in the room judge and critique the woman's worship of Jesus. But Jesus sees and affirms the beauty in her act, acknowledging it as deliberate and divine—rather than reckless. His voice cuts through the entire atmosphere, and he anoints her as *beautiful*. Regardless of what is said, thought, or felt about her, Jesus' loving, bold words finish the conversation. His words stand alone in the room. She need not even hear the prior rebukes of others. His words are enough.

Jesus *ends* our pursuit of beauty. When he affirms us, we have nowhere else to search. He pioneers, perfects, and finishes beauty in us. He releases us from our false productions and performances of beauty. In his presence, we are finally enough. Our race is over. All that has happened before, in shame and shortcomings, is erased. We are beautiful, anew.

REDEFINING BEAUTY

When we encounter Jesus' words, we find they are always good news. To unwrap the gift, we ought to ask: *what makes something, or someone, beautiful?*

Many identify beauty by what they *feel*. Beautiful things please us, induce awe, and draw crowds out of scattered societies. In museums, art exhibits capture people, arranging strangers in circles to loiter and bathe in the beauty before them. Beauty interrupts and seizes our attention. It incites curiosity in us. It beckons us to touch, stare, question, and grab. We long for these feelings to last, so we take pictures and write stories to remember. We share them over dinner. We look at photos, frame them, and look back again, and again.

The sensations of beauty are unmatched. We can discover great joy in them. We are wired to feel this way. But beauty is not just *feeling* in the conventional sense. Here, Jesus encourages us to expand our idea of beauty. He lifts our eyes beyond products and approval, to love and intimacy. To the Author of beauty. To ourselves.

And isn't that what true beauty always does? It reorients us to our true selves, in a way that we have missed, forgotten, or willfully turned from.

Save for their gender or age, many characters in the gospels are anonymous. We readers piece together their identities between scripture, commentaries, and culture. In this story, the only direct descriptor of this woman is that she is a woman. Elsewhere, we meet a bleeding woman defined by her illness and an adulteress defined by her sin. Here, we meet a woman defined by her love for Jesus. By writing the account of the events in this way, Mark identifies the woman with Jesus. Rather than overwhelm us with information about her upbringing, marital status, or occupation, we are forced to know her only by her interaction with Jesus.

"She has done a beautiful thing to me." – Mark 14:6 NIV

Despite our rushed, lacking introduction to this woman, she is quickly given a unique description, title, and legacy. Her identity is not determined by personality tests, interests, or her background, but by her actions. We often learn who people are, by how they exist and interact in the world. By the woman's actions, we learn of her feelings for Jesus. We learn that she loves him.

We learn that she was willing to endure the scoffing judgement of those present. And we learn that she has brought about God's very definition of *beauty*.

Though they can intersect, our notions of beauty are often starkly different from God's. What God saw as good in his creation, we saw as naked, profitable, and empty. Our clouded eyes drove us into new ways of living and subduing that only further collapsed our sense of beauty. But in spare moments, our eyes blink awake. In cradling a newborn child, savoring a grandmother's cooking, or sitting under a sweeping sunset, we see what Jesus sees: beauty.

For Jesus, beauty includes broken containers, surprise visits, radical generosity, and bold, disruptive behavior. His beauty has room for moments that are not put-together or curated, but unfinished, unrehearsed, and even unintended for display. When we share these moments, we are introduced to his beauty. When we are undone, performing for an audience of one. When we fall apart in front of our King.

BEGINNINGS OF BEAUTY

In this story, beauty is exclusively and intimately understood between the woman and Jesus. The others in the room did not understand the intention behind the woman's act, and judged it as inappropriate. But Jesus understood.

If beauty, in this way, does not deal with the opinions or perceptions of others, then we have found good news. Our pursuit of beauty is liberated. Beauty is not validated by onlookers—in fact, it may be overlooked and condemned by them. But it is legitimized by the Author of beauty himself. The quality of this woman's worship was not in its pomp or perfection. Her deed was neither practical nor even prudent. Its quality lay in its relationship. God called it *beautiful*, and so it was.

Beyond this moment, this is how the entire world begins: God calls it *good*, and it is so. This is also how beauty begins—from the mouth of our Maker. His creative framework involves naming things as good and beautiful—and so, they are. When we allow ourselves to hear the Creator's voice of beauty, we can be restored to our original existence.

Beauty is not a pursuit or a fleeting goal. God begins *and* finishes beauty.

Consider how our notions, obsessions, and quests for beauty drastically alter with this new paradigm. When we exchange our cheap pursuits for this, we will not need to flaunt, reason, or exhibit beauty. Our beauty will simply be, because God says it is so. And we will only be asked to accept and agree with it.

This creative framework grounds and corrects us, welding together our broken identities. We are designed to be satisfied by affirmation from our Creator alone. If we allow him, Jesus restores our clouded eyes to see ourselves as we are: masterpieces—declared beautiful, even before we are finished. We do not need to prove ourselves to him or others. In this holy moment, the grueling cycle of seeking approval is finally broken. He knows us. There is nothing left to convince, curate, or conceal.

BELOVEDNESS

The woman's act is not about grand gestures of romance. If beauty looks like a disrupted dinner or broken jar of perfume, it may also look like other things we may not imagine. A community's protest, a day of rest, or an awkward conversation, perhaps. In this story, God affirms beauty that is not necessarily exhibitional, but meaningful. Perhaps, a stranger's act of kindness, a lover's long-awaited embrace, or a mother's lullaby to her child.

These moments of intimacy are performed out of love, and only love. When we truly recognize beauty in ourselves or others, it is often accompanied by love. A person may find they are most beautiful when they love themselves the most. A person may feel beautiful when they similarly feel loved.

The woman's act, relationship, and identity of beauty is demonstrative of love. When we seek to embody, express, or experience beauty, we ought to question where *love* is present in the picture. When our beauty is a matter of social approval or commodification, there is no love in it. We cannot hope to be "beautiful" people, and all the while loathe ourselves.

If we are looking to beautify ourselves or create something beautiful, we do so knowing that we are loved. We are beautiful, made in the image of Beauty itself. We are beautiful because he calls us beautiful. And any endeavor we embark on concerning beauty begins and ends in our Creator's words—the only one with authority to define beauty. This is who we are, have been, and always will be. This is our identity. Amen.

"Then God said, 'Let us make mankind in our image, in our likeness…' God saw all that he had made, and it was very good." – Genesis 1: 26,31 NIV

03

On Beauty
and Generosity

She broke it. An unadulterated, expensive, fragrant perfume en-
cased in an alabaster jar for preservation—broken. Sealed and
saved for such a moment as this, the woman released the incense
to spill, soak, and saturate Jesus' hair, skin, and clothes. Her worship was not simply of words, but intimate, costly, and scrutinized
by those present. Their primary indictment? Efficiency.

*"Why this waste of perfume? It could have been sold for more than a year's
wages and the money given to the poor."* – Mark 14:4-5

The profound act of worship in Mark 14 was merely a waste, to
some. What leads the others in the room to such a hostile inter-
pretation of the woman's beautiful act? The forces of efficiency,
stinginess, and unbelief numb us to the possibility of generous,
beautiful worship.

THE ENEMY OF GENEROSITY

Efficiency asks questions of optimization, productivity, and waste. Our world is full of people aspiring to achieve maximal efficiency in work, parenting, dating—even ministry. Efficiency is a globally esteemed value, bred of market economies and human progress. In many cases, it is a helpful posture towards life. Efficiency loosens us into new ways of living, creating, and affecting change. And yet, the scriptures are full of anti-efficiency teachings and measures.

The Sabbath was given to the Israelites, whose lives had been ruthlessly reduced to pure production through hundreds of years of slavery. Dedicating one day away from work, for them, seemed a quite inefficient practice to implement in their newly liberated life. It did not align with their fractured identity. They were slaves—empty bodies valued solely by their productivity. But through the Sabbath, God invited them to live as free people in the structure of time he originally created.

When Jesus challenges our notions of efficiency, we might find ourselves hidden behind them. Like the Israelites, we may uncover issues of identity. We eagerly cloak insecurities, prejudices, and

anxieties with the guise of efficiency. And we deceive ourselves into thinking that we are, or simply need to be, highly efficient people.

The primary remedy prescribed in this story is generosity. Generosity—the readiness to give more than is expected. Generosity cuts through the colorless script of scarcity we often operate in. It jolts us awake. A generous gift, word, or service stirs us. Contrarily, efficiency stifles our sensitivity, need, and experiences of generosity altogether.

When the onlookers prompt the question, *"Why this waste of perfume,"* they reveal their idolatry of efficiency. Similar questions may have swirled around the room: *Why not just use a more appropriate amount? Why cause a scene? Why not just say something kind, instead of doing something controversial?* The scripture notes that the question of efficiency arose with anger and rebuke. To those present, the woman's act was unfair, disturbing, and, ultimately, foolish; it violated the common principles of efficiency and cut through their status quo.

We are not unlike them. This question of waste and efficiency is in the air we breathe, the water we drink. The woman's act prompts us to consider the voices, narratives, and values we regularly absorb by participating mentally, economically, and relationally in our world today.

HIDING BEHIND EFFICIENCY

The whole question of efficiency is predicated on the principle of scarcity. We strive to use assets "well," because assets are scarce. The others in the room interpreted the woman's act in economic terms. To them, it was a poor return on investment. They reduce her beautiful act of worship to a transaction, and assume some financial savvy would have improved it. They are not only wrong; they are hiding.

When we think of our money, possessions, and alabaster jars as limited resources, we cannot help but fall into this line of thinking. Throughout the scriptures, God repeatedly reminds us that his resources are *not* scarce. He makes our empty jars unending vessels of oil *(2 Kings 4)*. He turns a few fishes and loaves into a feast *(Mark 6)*. He gives us life itself, when we are merely dust *(Genesis 2)*.

The woman exhibited profound faith in God's generosity, by responding with generosity. She gave much, because she knew she had received much. The onlookers did not. Their distaste at her offering is not one of objective reasoning—it is a reaction that masks their inability to receive God's goodness. They argue that the incense would have better been sold, and the proceeds given to the poor. They are not only wrong; they are hiding.

Out of all those present at the table, Jesus had identified with, advocated for, and holistically loved the poor. Yet he took issue with their argument. They were not actually concerned with the poor. The woman's offering was simply so staggering that they resorted to virtue signaling rather than join her in worship.

When we consider "giving to the poor" in opposition to "giving to Jesus," we miss something. Charity is not a substitute to worship. It is an overflow of worship. What is our generosity to the poor actually worth, if not rooted in generosity to God? When we create this false dichotomy, we quickly substitute worship with good works. But an outward expression of compassion or justice is found first in love, faith, and generosity with Jesus.

God's economy does not work like ours. When we cheapen our relationship with Jesus into a transaction, and not a lavish date spent spoiling one another, we miss something. When we filter our offerings of money, time, and energy to God through a lens of scarcity, we miss something. And when our judgments on generosity align more with the world than with Jesus, we miss something.

WHAT IS JESUS WORTH?

"Then Judas Iscariot, one of the Twelve, went to the chief priests to betray Jesus to them. They were delighted to hear this and promised to give him money. So he watched for an opportunity to hand him over." – Mark 14:10-11 NIV

The woman is not alone in making an offering for Jesus. In sharp juxtaposition, Mark describes Judas Iscariot and the chief priests making a cheap bargain to arrest Jesus immediately after the woman's act. One gospel author [1] writes that Judas accepted 30 pieces of silver to hand Jesus over. *30 pieces.*

At the same table, we find two vastly different forces—the woman and Judas. Mark includes them together, to depict opposites. In a way, the bargain makes his betrayal worse. For Judas, a meager 30 pieces of silver is enough payment to betray Jesus. Rather than participate in God's plan for Jesus and the world, he attempts to end it.

If we desensitize and drift further from generous worship, we risk hardening ourselves into paths of temptation, betrayal, and re-bellion. Between Judas' bargain and the woman's offering, one question burns through the scripture: *What is Jesus worth?* A jar of perfume? 30 pieces of silver? In another scripture, Jesus himself answers the question.

"Jesus answered, 'If you want to be perfect, go, sell your possessions and give to the poor, and you will have treasure in heaven. Then come, follow me.'" – Matthew 19:21 NIV

To this woman, Jesus was worth *everything*. She had no reservations with her costly, prized perfume—likely worth a year's wages. She broke it. To her, generosity towards God was not a matter of quotas or percentages. She offers the entirety of herself and her possession.

We may not liken ourselves to Judas. But like the rest of those in the room that day, we can often be stingy with Jesus. We can consider time, lifestyles, or money as detached categories of which Jesus simply requires a cut of. We can despise his oversight, theologizing his teachings about our pockets to sit more comfortably with us. And in this isolated, irritable posture, we may miss that generosity is an experience of mutuality and relationship.

We rarely forget moments of generosity. When a friend or stranger is generous with us, we recognize the silent weight of it. It subverts and shakes our paradigms awake to new love, new space, and new life. The woman was generous in relationship to Jesus. We cannot fully experience generosity outside of relationship with God and others. It is deeply intertwined with our affection, worship, and participation in God and his kingdom.

As Jesus often described, the economy of the Kingdom of God has little to do with numbers—and everything to do with hearts. In Mark 12, Jesus says the poor widow who slipped two mites into the temple offering gave more than everyone else, even with their lavish gifts. Generosity is a heart posture and practice of relationship whereby we offer ourselves and our possessions to God.

Though we participate in a world economy and normality that sanctifies profit, greed, and efficiency, may we choose generosity. As we do, our identities and relationships will certainly flourish. Amen.

04

On Beauty
and Vulnerability

The world thickens our skin. To participate in society at creative, social, or civic levels requires some degree of invulnerability. Progress is depicted for us as a brute, self-centered *taking*, and performance involves masking ourselves. Proper guards and walls are constructed in order to avoid risk and harm. We mask. We harden. Despite an abundance of opportunities to showcase our lives and stories, we rarely lean into vulnerability. In this process, we become immune to beauty. But in Mark 14, the unnamed woman embodies vulnerability. In fact, it becomes a tool with which she risks much, expresses beauty, and communes with Jesus.

When we read the full chapter of Mark 14, we find that it begins on the day of the Feast of Passover. We overhear the chief priests and scribes callously devising how they might put Jesus to death in hushed whispers. At the end of this same day, Judas leaves Jesus' side to betray him to the same chief priests. Nestled in the middle of these profoundly hostile events is the story of the unnamed woman: a story so quiet in its power, yet resounding with transcendent beauty through vulnerability.

The woman's vulnerability offers us revealing access to Jesus' journey to the cross, in its beauty and mystery. She grasps his paradoxical ambition—to bring about real *and* ideal, vulnerability *and* power, freedom *and* sacrifice. In a moment of intense emotional exposure, she ventures vulnerably and alone into the beauty of the gospel, and the hidden nature of the Kingdom of God.

COSTLY VULNERABILITY

The experience of vulnerability leads us into suffering. The word "vulnerability" is derived from the Latin word *vulnerare*, meaning to *wound*. The definition includes "capable of being wounded" and "open to attack or damage." [1] The unnamed woman's departure into vulnerability risks everything for her—yet she boldly goes.

She enters into physical vulnerability, spending one year's wages on the oil and risking her well-being. She enters into emotional vulnerability, positioning herself at the center of ridicule and rejection. She enters into social vulnerability, as her presence as a woman and self-assertive act risks social condemnation. And she enters into spiritual vulnerability, acknowledging and acting upon an unwavering faith in the person and work of Jesus.

She enters the passion and suffering of Jesus, by identifying with his death through her costly and sacrificial gift. She creatively expresses her unwavering belief for all to witness. And through vulnerability, she ultimately enters into the beautiful mystery of Christ by prophetically anointing him—in life, for his future-death.

By anointing him with the incense, she identifies with Jesus' sacrifice on the cross—from her costly gift to her utter silence before her accusers. *Courageously*, she enters the room and disrupts an otherwise formal gathering. *Powerfully*, she breaks the jar over his head—the original Greek text implies she crushed the alabaster stone with her hands. And *lovingly*, she pours all the spikenard onto Christ. In the face of rebuke, her silence mirrors his own at the cross.

"He was oppressed and afflicted, yet he did not open his mouth; he was led like a lamb to the slaughter, and as a sheep before its shearers is silent, so he did not open his mouth." – Isaiah 53:7 NIV

The quietness of absolute acquiescence. Her vulnerability pairs itself with an unwavering certainty of knowing an un-knowable thing. Her act was a death to herself—the ultimate act of vulnerability.

"And they rebuked her harshly." – Mark 14:5 NIV

As the oil drips down his strands of hair, soaking into his beard, the critics cut through the affectionate silence. Their blame was not genuine, but a squirming escape from their own discomfort. The disarming work of vulnerability rattled them. They could not stand it.

INVISIBLE BEAUTY

A belief is only as strong as what you are willing to give for it. Vulnerability enables strong belief—yet demands a certain kind of openness—an open-handed and open-hearted living. It invites one to place themselves in harm's way, risking safety.

In this pivotal scene, Jesus was vulnerable. Enmity against him grew by the hour. By receiving the woman's lavish outpouring of love, he only risked his reputation and fate further. Still, he radiates power. In this moment, he disempowers and quiets his critics, acknowledging the beautiful thing she did. Yet, with his rebuke, he knowingly catalyzes a chain of events that end with his bloodied, broken body on a tree. For as Judas witnesses this powerful act of belief, his treacherous heart irreversibly turns.

The unnamed woman remains anonymous in the Gospel of Mark. Perhaps she had witnessed the miracle of Lazarus' resurrection, just days before. At the very least, she had heard of Jesus' reputation in Bethany for some time. Perhaps a special belief began to form—that he was more than merely a man. Perhaps she had heard of his other miracles, mingled with whispers of a looming death. However she came to know about Jesus, we can assuredly say that she loved him. She had "eyes to see and ears to hear," as he often spoke of. Her path was profoundly connected to his path, mission, and destination. And this path ultimately led to our collective redemption.

Jesus' disciples filtered much of his words through their own knowledge and pride. They reduced his purpose to a plain political potential, failing to understand his plan to redeem all things. Vulnerability requires that we open and offer our conceptions and understanding, inviting the expansive horizon of what might be. German writer Johann Wolfgang von Goethe said, "It is easier to perceive error than to find truth, for the former lies on the surface and is easily seen, while the latter lies in the depth, where few are willing to search for it." [2]

Could it be—that despite our passion for beauty, altars to beauty, and pursuits of beauty today—we rarely encounter *true* beauty? Our eyes may fix themselves around it, but never on it. Our ears may hear, but don't truly listen. In his stories, Jesus constantly alludes to inner beauty and hidden truth. And his students constantly miss it.

Because the unnamed woman came in vulnerability, the Lord met her in vulnerability. The symmetry of their vulnerability opened a realm of beauty that was otherwise invisible to everyone in the room.

"She has done a beautiful thing to me… Truly I tell you, wherever the gospel is preached throughout the world, what she has done will also be told, in memory of her." – Mark 14:6,9 NIV

We might imagine the thoughts and quarrels among those present, who quickly find their pride humbled by Jesus' rebuke. They are given a chance to peer into the same beauty as well. Whether they receive it or not, they will certainly no longer be the same. Jesus' words may impact them far into their lives.

In a world fixed on aesthetic beauty, vulnerability moves us beyond glamor. It peels back visible layers into an indefinite realm. An invisible reality—incomprehensible, and yet undeniably true. A completed world.

Of course, vulnerability is indeed costly and hardly glamorous. We are most susceptible to harm when we are vulnerable. We risk our reputation, being misunderstood, being taken advantage of, or even persecuted and oppressed. But to be vulnerable is to be open to what's on the other side of the veil of certainty. A beauty worth knowing, and worth risking it all for.

"For now we see only a reflection as in a mirror; then we shall see face to face. Now I know in part; then I shall know fully, even as I am fully known." – 1 Corinthians 13:12 NIV

In 1 Corinthians, Paul describes our life with Jesus as looking through a foggy, dark glass. We see outlines of shapes and cloudy shadows. We know it is real, but we cannot clearly see it. Still, we trust that it is worth knowing and risking for. Vulnerability, mixed with courage, enables us to enter that place of dim light and blurred edges, to eventually know and be fully known. Vulnerability leads us into beauty.

A VULNERABLE GOD

The next day, the smell likely lingered on his body as he broke bread and gave the cup to his disciples at Passover. The disciples would, against their own volition, experience the death of their friend and savior. They would soon deny Jesus, run, and hide. It wasn't unlike them.

The disciples often stood under a veneer of denial, avarice, self-importance, criticism, and misunderstanding. Jesus often rebuked them for their hardened hearts and inability to see, hear, and understand. They wanted a savior that was *invulnerable*. They valued their own security, permanence, and impenetrable ideals over the things Jesus prioritized. They yearned for a political ruler to forcibly usurp the Roman empire. But in God's inverted Kingdom, suffering is mixed with glory, the last becomes first, outsiders become insiders, and true life flourishes from death. Such a kingdom is a wildly vulnerable enterprise.

To participate in God is to participate in vulnerability. But it is a worthy path. The beauty of the woman's vulnerability has lasting effects. It paints boldly on our otherwise bleak world, leaving a masterpiece in its wake.

The table is alive today. Jesus quietly awaits for us to join him. To follow Jesus is to be vulnerable. Our lives will inevitably be marked by costly suffering. But it is a worthy path. On it, we will discover breathtaking beauty. May we choose the way of vulnerability. Amen.

05

On Beauty
and Mystery

A bristling galaxy, a sunlit horizon, a new birth, *love*. The most beautiful moments of the human experience are indisputably cloaked in mystery and wonder.

Beauty, at first, perks our senses. Our senses serve as signals; with them, we are designed to encounter, enjoy, and create beauty. And still—our senses can only grasp so much. We can only see so many colors, hear so many frequencies, and understand so many things. Our senses, in some cases, can even mislead us and prove insufficient for understanding the world.

God's sense of beauty is, at best, mysterious. Though we may never fully understand it, our call to follow God involves contemplating and participating in such beauty. In Mark 14, Jesus helps us see beauty—and marvel at the mystery of it, with or without understanding.

GIVING TO THE GIVER

The incarnate, relational, salvific journey of Jesus is replete with glorious things—and yet, this is the only occasion that Jesus calls something *beautiful*. We are led to ask: what makes this moment so different?

The crux of the gospels involves Jesus encountering, redeeming, and restoring humanity. He fulfills our needs. He heals lepers, calms storms, and exorcises demons. But in this story, the woman fulfills *his* "need" by anointing Jesus for his looming death. She enters into a mystery that is otherwise invisible—yet as real as the jar she breaks. She takes initiative to love Jesus and participate in his destiny. In her act, she is not playing the role of a recipient.

The mystery is this: How might we offer anything to an omnipotent, omniscient, and omnipresent God? How do we give to the Giver of life itself? Though the notion seems irrational, we find that God regularly invites humanity to *give* to him. Just as God gave to the Israelites, the Israelites gave firstfruits in return, sharing in a mutual covenant. Today, God invites us to give toward himself—through the church, the poor, and in worship. In Mark 14, the woman gives not because she is required to—but because she longs to.

"She has done a beautiful thing to me… Truly I tell you, wherever the gospel is preached throughout the world, what she has done will also be told, in memory of her." – Mark 14:6,9 NIV

As she gives, she receives a lofty affirmation. One that no other character in the gospels has heard from Jesus' lips. He crowns her with specific, sacred language. The One who first called anything *tov* (good), now calls her act *kalos*—beautiful as an outward sign of an inward goodness.

We cannot grasp the mystery of giving to the Giver, but we do know that it is a mystery worth exploring. As we give, we embody beauty, enjoy intimate connection with God, and join the lengthy, global experience of redemption.

Though the disciples often argued about who would sit at Jesus' right hand, it is the unnamed woman who Jesus privileges with supreme attachment to his gospel and legacy. While his own disciples fail to accept his death, this woman independently prepares him for it.

FEARING AMBIGUITY

If we had been standing in the room when Jesus was anointed, we might very well have stood alongside the crowd in confusion, disgust, and doubt. We would have questions. Even now, thousands of years later, we *still* have questions.

Why is the woman breaking a jar of perfume, traditionally used as a dowry? Why does Jesus say, "The poor you will always have with you, but you will not always have me?" Out of all the stories of the gospels, why does Jesus call this "beautiful?"

With our retrospective understanding of Jesus' death and burial, we might answer some of these questions. But to the onlookers, the moment was absolutely mysterious.

Mystery lives in the ambiguous pockets of our lived experiences. Mystery does not make sense in the moment, and hardly does afterwards. It is veiled often as irrational, illogical, and incoherent. Our bodily response involves confusion, indignation, or frustration. We fear ambiguity.

Our world prizes rationalism and reductionism. We adore individuals who can capture complexity and reduce it to something simple—giving us one-liner, bite-sized meanings to fit within the racing, cluttered chaos of our lives. This skill is worthy of admiration, and increasingly important for a society with decreasing attention spans. However—it is not where mystery lives.

Theologian Eugene Peterson once said, "Beauty is not the absence of meaning, but the presence of more meaning than we can comprehend." [1] To comprehend requires deep time, focus, and value—and even then, there is no guarantee that we can truly grasp the meaning of a mysterious or mystical experience.

Nonetheless, the story of the woman with the alabaster jar invites us toward mystery. It calls us to trust in God, even when we cannot comprehend what he is doing. It invites us to a greater perspective of our creative, beautiful identity and purpose in the world. And it is an invitation to leave behind our cloudy conceptions, and trust in God's sense of beauty.

Mystery is never a popular road. If you consider exploring it, you will be departing from the norm. You must accept your inability to comprehend, articulate, and embody the mystery of God. Similar to the crowd in the room, there will be naysayers and critics poised to dismiss and discredit you at every turn. But the invitation remains: enter into mystery, just as the woman did. It is good and well, even when things do not make sense. And we will find God there.

WONDER

While we normally associate mystery with confusion, a more appropriate response would be *wonder*.

We are bloated with instant gratification, unparalleled access to knowledge, and wealth beyond our moral capacity. We clinically categorize reality, ingesting life as a series of problems and questions—to which we have, or *will* have, all the answers. This, perhaps, is why our primary response to mystery evokes the foggy feeling of confusion. Flustered, we lose ourselves—because we have sewn ourselves together with "answers." We have all but lost our ability to be awed in wonder. And we have all but lost *ourselves* in the process.

If God is anything, he is mysterious. The things of God are mysterious. Our pools of knowledge pale beside the oceans of what we do not yet understand. And though societal progress naturally pushes us to deeper understanding and breakthroughs, we should not lose our ability to awe. We should not grow unfamiliar with our limitations. We should not, like the others in the room, respond to mystery with quick, hazy judgments.

Artists are among the few who still maintain their relationship with wonder. Any practiced creative is well-acquainted with their own limitations. And any honest creative has prioritized wonder in their practice. For many, we are the mouthpieces and conduits for wonder. Our work captures our own wonder, and elicits wonder from others.

Awe and wonder are appropriate responses to mystery. Beauty, above all else, calls forth wonder. As beauty-makers, we are invited to help rekindle wonder in the human body and soul. Like much of creation, our creations will reflect mystery. The human response to mystery will involve welcoming limitations, calming the anxiety of confusion, and simply practicing wonder.

Wonder can transform our world. When we experience it, we concede our powers of analysis and answer. We incline ourselves toward mystery rather than away from it. And we rediscover our humanity, in light of what we cannot explain—not what we can. As beauty moves us to wonder, it renders our humanity humble, healed, and hungry for mystery.

THE WAY OF GOD

God is familiar with mystery. Throughout the scriptures, he uses nonlinear, illogical, mysterious ways to engage with humanity.

He incarnates into his own creation. He enters through the body of a young, poor woman, in circumstances unfit for royalty. He makes his home among the world's least, not the elite. He preaches of a kingdom predicated on sacrificial love and eternal life, rather than empire. He dies a criminal's death while being a perfectly pure, holy individual. And he teaches that in order to experience *true* life, you must lose it. If it is anything, God's work of incarnation, resurrection, and redemption is teeming with mystery.

This divine mystery creates paradox, doubt, and conflict for many—even during Jesus' time. But for others—like the curious Nicodemus or lonely Samaritan woman—it creates beauty. It captures their hearts, souls, and lives—reaching into their families, cities, and destinies. There is an utterly confounding power in mystery.

Though there is much that is inexplicable and mysterious about us, we are not creatures of mystery. We live and die by linearity. Our everyday patterns of human life, understanding, and work have been developed to help us navigate terrifying realities.

Here, the woman's example snaps us out of a sleepy status quo. When she breaks the jar and pours the perfume, he recognizes her language immediately: mystery. She participates in the nonlinear, mystical, secretive way of Jesus—and he affirms it as *beautiful*.

Like the woman, we can choose mystery. God's narrative will inevitably involve it, as it always has. If we desire to participate in the creative work of God, we have to be comfortable with the uncomfortable prospect of mystery. We have to exercise wonder. In doing so, we join a long legacy of faithful individuals and groups committed to embracing the way that leads, albeit obscurely, to eternal life. Amen.

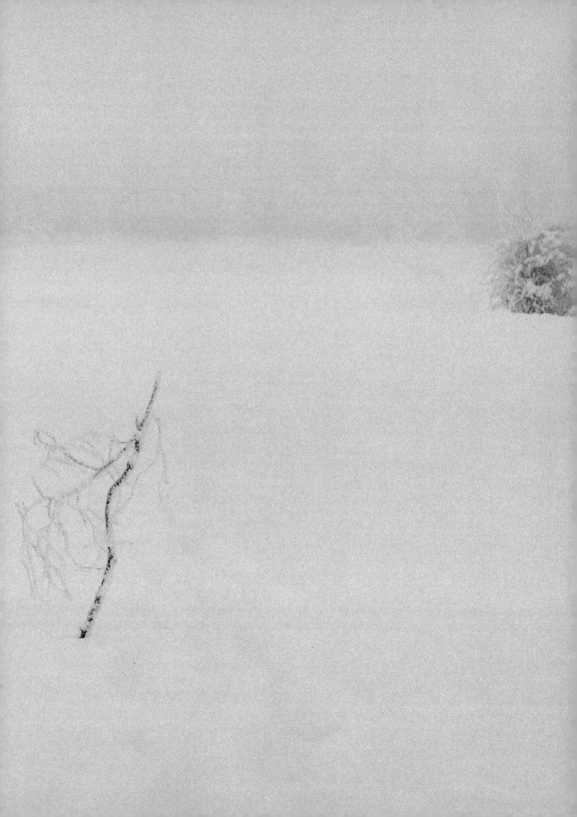

06

On Beauty
and Justice

We are often led to believe that the ideals of beauty and justice are conflicting rivals, incapable of occupying the same space—let alone supporting one another. This notion of separation is implicit in the ways we treat and value each.

Beauty often improperly functions as a pretentious distraction—rather than an advocate for justice. In our world, beauty seems to be a matter of stuffy showrooms—while justice appears as a matter of human rights. In Mark 14, the crowds' indignant response to the woman speaks to this strident divide between beauty and justice.

When we hear Jesus' response, we are urged to reexamine this supposed separation. Beauty may not, in fact, be irrelevant to justice. When practiced well, we might find beauty is both a primer and characteristic of justice. It lies at the crux of meaningful justice-making in our world, and the two are designed to work in unison. And perhaps, we may never even actualize justice without the sensuous, imaginative, soulful experience of beauty.

BEAUTY AS THE PRIMER FOR JUSTICE

Beauty as Movement

Consider the moments in life that we deem worthy of calling: *beautiful*. The birth of a child, perhaps. A delightful feast with loved ones. An unexpected act of sacrificial care. In moments like these, we are, quite literally, *moved*. Awed by new life and love in the child, we are moved to tears of joy. In the feast, we are moved towards laughter and warmth by those around us. And in receiving an act of sacrificial care, we are compelled to act sacrificially ourselves. Beauty moves us. Beautiful moments in our lives propel us into response—they never stagnate us. And we are never the same again.

When these beautiful moments echo toward movements of justice, they create ripples of change—for ourselves, our communities, and our entire world. Beauty is a necessary spark for justice to begin. A particularly poignant poem might shake us out of apathy. A gripping mural may compel us to resist oppression. A radiant garden may inspire our dreams for a renewed world. Beauty calls us inward, toward God, and toward each other— and in doing so, organically calls forth justice.

Good News to the Poor

"The poor you will always have with you, and you can help them any time you want. But you will not always have me… Truly I tell you, wherever the gospel is preached throughout the world, what she has done will also be told, in memory of her." – Mark 14:7,9 NIV

At the time, anyone who knew Jesus knew he loved the poor. When those in the room voice their complaints, they intended to weaponize his just gospel against the woman. Picture the puzzlement on their faces when he rejects their proposal. Even for us, these words from Jesus sit uncomfortably against our notions of nobility, charity, and him. After all, Jesus centers his *entire* mission on the poor, as declared in the *Nazarene Manifesto*.

"The Spirit of the Lord is on me, because he has anointed me to proclaim good news to the poor. He has sent me to proclaim freedom for the prisoners and recovery of sight for the blind, to set the oppressed free, to proclaim the year of the Lord's favor." – Luke 4:18-19 NIV

When Jesus corrects the crowd, he is not arguing against charity or justice. He is opening their eyes. He declares that a deeper, initial kindling must occur with ourselves and God before justice can truly roll forward. Here, the woman exemplifies the necessary precondition for justice: beauty. And the "good news to the poor" that Jesus offers is intertwined with and catalyzed by this woman's act. Without beauty, justice lacks substance and purpose. It dies, hollow and lifeless. But beauty provides a crucial container for the "good news" of justice to be carried out throughout the world.

Those of us who are *justice carriers* are invited to remember that justice does not exist in a vacuum. Justice exists to make a more beautiful, whole world. Beauty can initiate justice, and serve as markers for it. Our work will be sustained by remembering this connection.

Those of us who are *beauty-makers* are invited to direct our making toward acts of justice. Our creative practice must be bent toward the service of humanity. We are invited to spark vision and kindle the imagination for justice. We call it forward.

As we work together to imagine, create, and do justice, our interconnected pursuit of *Shalom*, a vision of wholeness, can thrive.

BEAUTY AND THE MARGINS

Jesus sits with lepers. He eats with tax-collectors. He restores sight to the blind. He restores hearing to the deaf. He feeds the hungry. He welcomes the outcast. He forgives the sinful.

The story of Jesus is one of advocating for those on the margins—regardless of ethnicity, gender, disability, or socioeconomic status. Jesus displaces himself in the service of others.

As human beings, we are predisposed toward self-centeredness. We obsess over our own self-preservation. Our books, films, and media emboldens self-improvement, and we are easily self-absorbed in our own needs and wants. In the West, the successful individual is hailed and prized before the collective. Our culture idolizes *self*.

Biblical justice involves the literal act of removing oneself from the center of attention, society, or influence. In justice, we choose—with empathy and compassion—to place the needs of another before our own. We voluntarily place ourselves on the margins, choosing to bring the poor, prisoner, and oppressed to the center of our collective story.

So, how do we, as naturally self-centered humans, deliberately pull ourselves to the margins in service of another? Beauty offers us a doorway.

Consider, again, your experience with things you would deem: beautiful. This time, perhaps, a painting or artwork that pleases you. In the moment that you experience it, the painting becomes the center of your focus. You let your guard down. Any preoccupations and self-interests fall away as you immerse yourself in the beauty of the piece.

When we witness something beautiful, beauty de-centers us. It takes center-stage. We voluntarily place ourselves at its margin, elevating beauty to the center of our world. And at this less obvious "margin," we are more attentive to others.

Living Justly

As Christians, we are called to break our inherent self-centeredness. God calls us to serve and give generously, seeing the needs of others as our own, and advocating for those on the margins. Rather than performing occasional acts of justice, we are called to live a holistic life of justice. But this call is also full of limitations. We cannot sustain this others-centered lifestyle alone. *Living justly* requires Jesus. We must experience his beauty to help take us out of ourselves, and into justice. Without it, we experience burnout and lose purpose.

Here, the woman experiences beauty in Jesus. Overcome with passion and awe, she sacrifices her own comfort and reputation to radically love Jesus. She places him at the center—an act that he calls *beautiful*.

By placing Jesus at the center of our lives, we can best center others as well. As he describes in Matthew 25, Jesus identifies himself with those on the margins. When we care for them, we care for him. Centering Jesus in our daily lives is no easy task, but in doing so, we are led to see his image in those on society's margins. And we are similarly led to center them, as well.

Justice is best practiced when it is not a partisan ploy, emotional endeavor, or self-seeking strategy—but when it starts with Jesus as the central authority, partner, and spirit.

ENGAGING THE IMAGINATION

In an interview, theologian Walter Brueggemann discusses beauty and justice in the prophetic scriptures, saying: "...we only talked about the prophets as moral teachers. There was no attention to the artistic, aesthetic quality of how they did that. But it is the only way in which you can think outside of the box. Otherwise, passion for justice just becomes another ideology, and it does not have transformative power... I think a great temptation [amongst those] who care about justice is to reduce it to a formula... and then the poetry comes and breaks that open again." [1]

Biblical justice is *beautiful*. It is depicted in breathtaking, illustrative stories, it is articulated in gripping poetry, and it is purposed with a beautiful goal: *Shalom*. It splits open our metallic, perfunctory paradigms and frameworks, and calls forth a greater perspective.

In our methodology of justice-making, we may quickly forget the potential and importance of engaging the imagination. We cannot always practice just living, because we cannot always imagine such a reality. Our imaginations are burdened by horrific injustice, with no foreseeable hope.

French philosopher Simone Weil says, "The horror of poverty is essentially a horror of ugliness." [2] Most often, an oppressor's injustice is tied to their prejudice, distaste, and disgust for a group. They see an *other* in their neighbor—not themselves or their God. Their hearts are hardened to the inherent beauty in those they oppress.

The oppressed struggle similarly. When impoverished or disenfranchised communities fail to imagine themselves in a liberated, healed way of living, they cannot be empowered into it. They retreat to compliance and defeat. Their oppressive contexts steal their sense of beauty, and extinguish signs of it in and around them.

We cannot minimize the importance of beauty as guideposts of justice. Beauty melts our hardened hearts, providing a necessary language for justice to be spoken and heard. We need our acts of justice to be beautiful—not merely formulaic or strategic. Oppressors must reckon with the beauty in their neighbor, if they are to remove themselves from the center and elevate those on the margins. And the oppressed must be sensitized to the beauty in and around them, and empowered to imagine a more beautiful future.

This is no small work, but it is necessary. May we follow the example of the woman, who embodies sincerity, care, gentleness, and genuineness. She imagines an unforeseeable future, and partners with Jesus in the ultimate work of justice. Amen.

07

On Beauty
and Changing
the World

"How beautiful are the feet of those who bring good news!" – Romans 10:15 NIV

Dirty, bruised, and misspent, to some. To the prophet Isaiah, the feet of gospel-carriers are beautiful. The scriptures have always associated the gospel with beauty. In Mark 14, Jesus confirms it with his own words when he calls her act *beautiful.* To further make his point, he crowns her with another lofty compliment.

"Wherever the gospel is preached throughout the world, what she has done will also be told, in memory of her." – Mark 14:9

The unnamed woman is the only person in all the scriptures who receives such exaltation from Jesus. The Author of life himself wants her story to be written alongside his—and he considers *beauty* the most appropriate supplement to his gospel.

As we let Jesus' words permeate our hearts, we are led to ask—along with those present—*why?* Why is beauty so intimately interwoven with the gospel? Why will beauty proliferate throughout the world? What role does beauty play in God's redemptive, creative plan? As we lean into his language, we might find that beauty is central to changing the world.

BEAUTY AS CALLING

Jesus follows his declaration of *beautiful* with a description of this woman's destiny. Her act is to be shared throughout the world. As he describes the prophetic legacy of her actions, he speaks to the sacred marriage of beauty and calling. They are one together, deeply integrated. Beauty as calling. Beauty calling us into our highest selves. Beauty as essential to our calling.

Irish poet John O'Donohue reflects on this connection in an interview, saying, "[Beauty is] not a neutral thing, but it's actually calling you. And I feel that one could write a wonderful psychology just based on the notion of being called—being called to yourself and called to transfigure what has hardened or got wounded within you." [1]

Beauty begets beauty. It is hardly static, shallow, or meaningless. It calls to those listening, watching, and feeling. It reaches beyond our rationalized numbness, and grabs *something*. Depth. Soul. Being. And as we allow it, we might find that beauty contributes to our healing, becoming, and creativity.

The woman's act is calling out to those around her. Perhaps we too, like them, are also stuffed, seated at the table, and stumped by this act of worship. Perhaps we too need Jesus to explain it to us. And perhaps we too are also called to crack, pour, and drain our own precious jars.

When Jesus says, "She did what she could," he uses the word *epoiēsen*, which means to make, manufacture, or construct. She was not thoughtlessly exhausting her savings—but actively constructing and creating something. She was joining God's redemptive artwork, which climaxed in Jesus' death and resurrection. The unnamed woman was an artist, an architect, and a genius. Though Jesus was surrounded by professionals, thinkers, and zealots, it was the unnamed woman who first embraces the substance of *calling*.

BEAUTY AND THE GOSPEL

Today, we ask many questions of faith: *Is it still relevant? Is it still real? How do we practice it?* We engage with faith as archaic, text-heavy doctrines or trendy, adapted content to fit within our public screen. We see it in study, strategy, and results. But we rarely ask: *Is it beautiful?*

Not beauty in the simple, surface-level sense of decoration and appeal. Beauty in the deeper sense. Beauty as art, identity, generosity, vulnerability, mystery, justice, and destiny. Beauty as food, play, and rest for the soul. Beauty as wonder and future-making. Beauty as restoring all of creation and humanity to its original condition.

Here, Jesus elevates beauty to a towering importance alongside his story. He declares beauty as a primary descriptor of his gospel work and news to the world. Beauty and the gospel are inseparable. And when we let this woman's example compel us, we are taking her place alongside the gospel of Jesus. We are loving Jesus, joining him in his redemptive work, and ultimately co-creating the world as it ought to be—beautiful.

Law of Fruitfulness

"God blessed them and said to them, 'Be fruitful and increase in number; fill the earth and subdue it. Rule over the fish in the sea and the birds in the sky and over every living creature that moves on the ground.'" – Genesis 1:28 NIV

The first command given to humanity is the law of fruitfulness: *be fruitful*. This mandate permeates through all of history. In the face of oppression, desolation, and great pressure, God blesses individuals and communities to be fruitful. Jesus regularly encourages his followers to *bear fruit*.

Throughout the scriptures, we see an innately contagious, spreading, amplifying quality in the good news of Jesus. When one ostracized woman drinks of it, she invites her whole town to do the same—defying all her preexisting confines. This is the nature

of *good news*, or the gospel: it demands to be shared, shouted, and spread. The gospel also operates by the law of fruitfulness, through faithfulness. This multiplicative quality is also evident in beauty.

English poet John Keats writes, "A thing of beauty is a joy for ever: its loveliness increases; it will never pass into nothingness." [2] Beauty begets beauty. Though our eyes tire and memories dwindle, beauty expands in obvious and unseen ways.

In an interview, animation director Hayao Miyazaki recalls a visit to the Tate Modern in London. When he saw the painting *Ophelia* by John Everett Milias, he was so transfixed by the image that it drove him to completely change the aesthetic of his subsequently award-winning film, *Ponyo*. [3]

Why do artists go to art galleries? In part, it is because these hallways are brimming with inspiration. With the inspirational, arousing quality of art, artists can quickly discover doorways into their own beauty. When we witness beauty, we want to make beauty ourselves.

Law of Timelessness

We have often heard it said, "Beauty is in the eye of the beholder." Though the statement has many implications, one is particularly strong: beauty is timeless and boundless.

A natural mountain range will never cease to be beautiful, because a city-dwelling boy will one day have his breath stolen by it. A compelling art piece will never cease to be beautiful, because an art student will one day find herself gripped by it. An old, acoustic song cover will never cease to be beautiful, because an aspiring singer will one day reap great inspiration from it.

Though we tend to wrap limits around beauty like time, popularity, and relevance, there is no objective way of determining

when beauty *ends*. It is an experience between an individual and a creative work. As creatives, we should form our work with timelessness in mind.

When we send our creativity out into the world, we do not know its effects. We cannot be certain of who it reached, and what it affected. And we cannot gauge its true power. The gospel is similar. When we live, practice, and share it, the effects are immeasurable. Though the *narrow road* that Jesus offers seems futile and impractical, it leads to eternal life. Though we lose our lives, we gain them.

To the onlookers, the woman's art was *apoleia*—a complete waste and loss. To Jesus, it was *kalos*—beautiful, an outward sign of inward good. Divine beauty and goodness will never be properly understood or affirmed in this life. Our participation in God's beautiful plan will appear as waste and foolishness to others. But as we partake in it, we join an eternal legacy alongside his gospel.

CREATIVE POWER

It is no coincidence that our faith begins with creation and beauty. The holy precedent of Genesis screams to us through all the other scriptures, up to the very breath of this moment: God is creating. We have been invited to join the dance.

Creation is the unifying rhythm of all the world. We are prone to reduce, commodify, and destroy—but beauty reminds us that we are also designed to create, compose, and cultivate. This woman's beautiful legacy beckons us to consider how we are involved in God's creative cosmic work. It demonstrates how beauty slices, disrupts, and confronts our status quo. It tells of how beauty is costly—a generous gift amidst great criticism and opposition. And it embodies the selfless, soulful art which connects us to ourselves, others, and our Creator.

Here, Jesus privileges beauty-making to have cosmic purpose and potential. Just as God created all of a beautiful world, we are sent to co-create and re-create a beautiful world. As creatives, we contain an imaginative capacity to see unseen beauty—and usher others into it.

Changing the world involves the original framework of creation. It is not a different task altogether. It is not an endeavor dominated by intellectual elites, political platforms, or market power. It is ultimately a creative work. It begins in the deepest fabric of humanity—the kind accessed only by beauty. It is an experiential, imaginative creating of a present and distant reality that we all, in some sense, identify with. It is the grand enterprise of worldbuilding, and the humble warmth of homemaking, wrapped into one. It is soul, longing, sacrifice, wonder, and hope. It is *beautiful*.

May we consider beauty as an essential element of the change that we ache to witness in the land of the living. Amen.

 ALABASTER

EDITOR-IN-CHIEF
& HEAD OF WRITING
Daniel Sunkari

WRITERS
Adaobi Ugoagu (Ch. 5)
Alana Freitas (Ch. 2)
Bryan Ye-Chung (Ch. 1, 6)
Daniel Sunkari (all)
Evie Shaffer (Ch. 4)

STUDIO PHOTOGRAPHER
Samuel Han

PHOTOGRAPHERS
Ian Teraoka
Jacob Chung
Mason Boni
Mike Sunu
Salomé Watel
Samuel Han

LAYOUT DESIGN
Kristy Cheng

CONTENT ASSISTANT
Darin McKenna

STUDIO ASSISTANT
Daniel Han

CO-FOUNDER
& CREATIVE DIRECTOR
Bryan Ye-Chung

CO-FOUNDER
& BUSINESS DIRECTOR
Brian Chung

OPERATIONS DIRECTOR
Willa Jin

PRODUCT MANAGER
Tyler Zak

CUSTOMER EXPERIENCE
SPECIALIST
Emaly Hunter

COVER IMAGE
Tyler Zak

ENDNOTES

ON BEAUTY AND ART

1. Brueggemann, Walter. Living toward a Vision: Biblical Reflections on Shalom. United Church Press, 1984.
2. Martin, Agnes. Writings. Cantz, 1992.
3. Nouwen, Henri J. M. You Are the Beloved: Daily Meditations for Spiritual Living. Convergent Books, 2017.

ON BEAUTY AND GENEROSITY

1. Matthew 26:14-15.

ON BEAUTY AND VULNERABILITY

1. Brown, Brené. Daring Greatly: How the Courage to Be Vulnerable Transforms the Way We Live, Love, Parent and Lead. Avery, 2015.
2. Goethe, Johann Wolfgang von. Maxims and Reflections. Enhanced Media Publishing, 2017.

ON BEAUTY AND MYSTERY

1. Peterson, Eugene. Twitter, Twitter, 12 Sept. 2015, twitter.com/petersondaily/status/642753109798875136?lang=en.

ON BEAUTY AND JUSTICE

1. Krista Tippett, and Walter Brueggemann, In the Room with Walter Brueggemann (Live Stream), On Being Project, 2011, www.youtube.com/watch?v=qAMnq4vdDvE&.
2. Weil, Simone. Waiting for God. Routledge &; K. Paul, 1951.

ON BEAUTY AND CHANGING THE WORLD

1. O'Donohue, John. "The Inner Landscape of Beauty." The On Being Project, 31 Aug. 2017, onbeing.org/programs/john-odonohue-the-inner-landscape-of-beauty-aug2017/#transcript.
2. Keats, John. Endymion & the Longer Poems of John Keats. J M Dent and Co, Aldine House, 1905.
3. Miyazaki, Hayao. "Ep. 1 Ponyo Is Here - 10 Years with Hayao Miyazaki: NHK WORLD-JAPAN On Demand." NHK WORLD, 2019, www3.nhk.or.jp/nhkworld/en/ondemand/video/3004569/.

WWW.ALABASTERCO.COM